# THE ADVENTURES OF TWO DUTCH DOLLS AND A "GOLLIWOGG"

# LECTOR HOUSE PUBLIC DOMAIN WORKS

This book is a result of an effort made by Lector House towards making a contribution to the preservation and repair of original classic literature. The original text is in the public domain in the United States of America, and possibly other countries depending upon their specific copyright laws.

In an attempt to preserve, improve and recreate the original content, certain conventional norms with regard to typographical mistakes, hyphenations, punctuations and/or other related subject matters, have been corrected upon our consideration. However, few such imperfections might not have been rectified as they were inherited and preserved from the original content to maintain the authenticity and construct, relevant to the work. We believe that this work holds historical, cultural and/or intellectual importance in the literary works community, therefore despite the oddities, we accounted the work for print as a part of our continuing effort towards preservation of literary work and our contribution towards the development of the society as a whole, driven by our beliefs.

We are grateful to our readers for putting their faith in us and accepting our imperfections with regard to preservation of the historical content. We shall strive hard to meet up to the expectations to improve further to provide an enriching reading experience.

Though, we conduct extensive research in ascertaining the status of copyright before redeveloping a version of the content, in rare cases, a classic work might be incorrectly marked as not-in-copyright. In such cases, if you are the copyright holder, then kindly contact us or write to us, and we shall get back to you with an immediate course of action.

**HAPPY READING!**

# THE ADVENTURES OF TWO DUTCH DOLLS AND A "GOLLIWOGG"

## BERTHA UPTON

ISBN: 978-93-5342-655-2

First Published:                    -

LECTOR HOUSE LLP
E-MAIL: lectorpublishing@gmail.com

# THE ADVENTURES OF TWO DUTCH DOLLS AND A "GOLLIWOGG"

BY

BERTHA UPTON

ILLUSTRATED
BY
FLORENCE K. UPTON

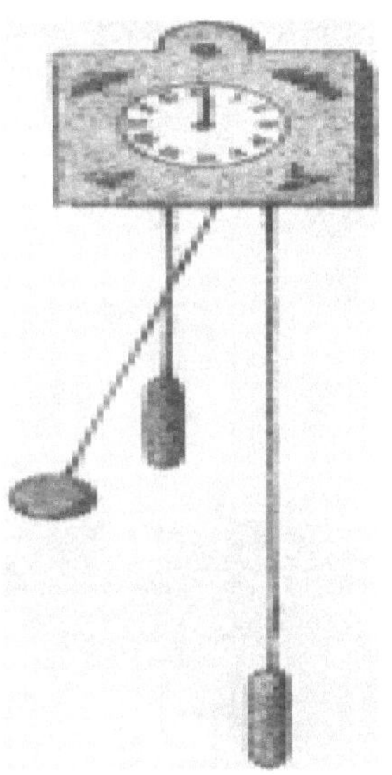

'Twas on a frosty Christmas Eve
When Peggy Deutchland woke
From her wooden sleep
On the counter steep
And to her neighbour spoke,

"Get up! get up, dear Sarah Jane!
Now strikes the midnight hour,
When dolls and toys
Taste human joys,
And revel in their power.

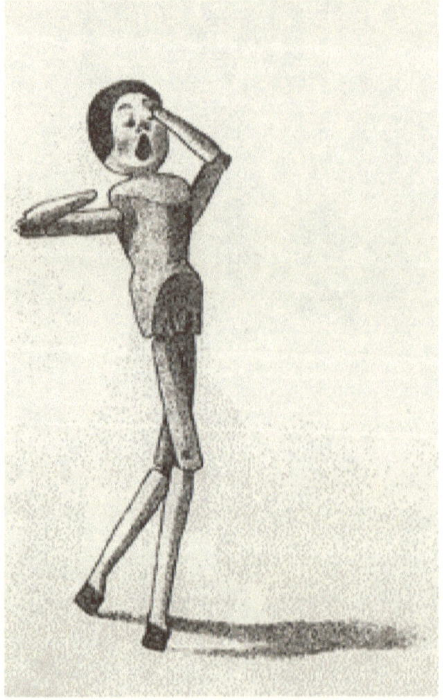

I long to try my limbs a bit,
And you must walk with me;
Our joints are good
Though made of wood,
And I pine for liberty.

For twelve long months we've lain in here.
But we don't care a fig;

When wide awake
It does not take
Us long to dance a jig.

But who comes here across our path,
In gay attire bedight?
A little girl
With hair in curl,
And eyes so round and bright.

Good evening Miss, how fine you look,
Beside you I feel bare;
I must confess
I need a dress
If I would look as fair.

On that high pole I see a flag
With colors red and blue;
Dear Sarah Jane
'Tis very plain
A climb you'll have to do.

You're young and light--so now be quick
Dear sister good and kind;
You look dismayed
Don't be afraid,
It's not so hard you'll find.

Then up the pole with trembling limbs,
Poor Sarah Jane did mount;
She dared not lag,
But seized the flag,
Ere you could twenty count.

Big Peggy gazed with deep concern,
And mouth wide open too;
Her only care
That she might wear
A gown of brilliant hue.

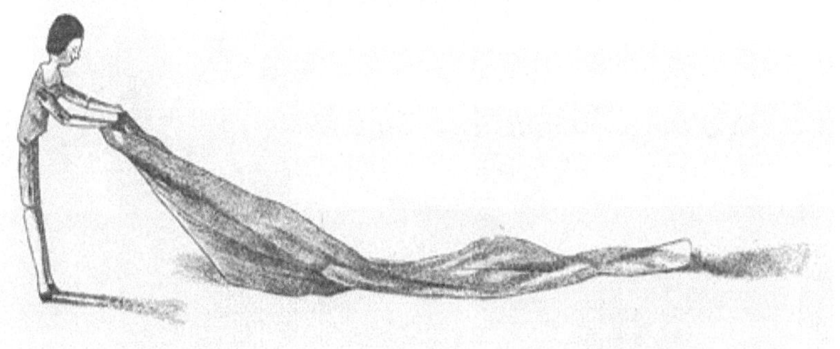

Now Peg' by instinct seemed to know

Where scissors might be got;
The "fits" were bad,
But then she had
No patterns on the spot.

Soon where the garments hurried on;
Sarah looked well in blue;
Mirror in hand
She took her stand,
While Peggy pinned her's through.

Said Peggy--"After work so hard,
I think a rest we need;
Let's take a ride
Seated astride
Upon this gentle steed."

Then simple Sarah Jane climbed up
Upon his wooden back;
With tim'rous heart
She felt him start
Upon the open track.

Ere long they knew that hidden there,
Beneath a stolid mien,
Dwelt a fierce will.
They could not still
They rode as if by steam!

Peggy held on with tightening grip,
While Sarah Jane behind,
Having no hold
To make her bold,
To screaming gave her mind.

"O Peggy! put me down I pray!
I ride in mortal dread!
Do make him stop,
Or I shall drop
And break my wooden head!"

E'en as those piteous words she spoke,
They struck a fearful "snag"
Their grips they lost,
And both were tossed
Upon the cruel "flag".

Their senses for a moment gone,
They lay in ghastly plight;
Their fiery steed
From burden freed,
Maintained his onward flight.

Then each in aching consciousness
Rose slowly with sad groans;
Next faced about
With angry shout,
Followed by tears and moans.

Each blamed the other for the fall;

Until, in gentler mood,
Their hurts they dress,
While both confess
The crying did them good.

A wooden crutch poor Peggy finds
To help her on her feet;
Both solemn-faced
Their steps retraced
To where they first did meet.

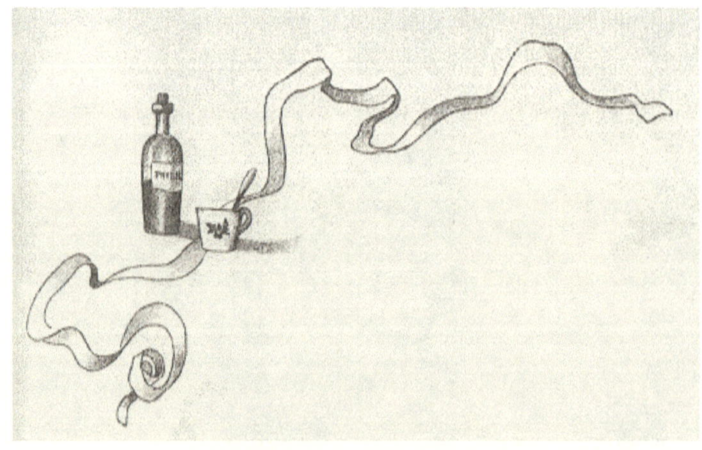

But sorrow's tears are quickly dried
With dolls as well as men.--
A jolly crowd
All laughing loud
(I think you'll count just ten.)

Mounted a little wooden cart,
While Peggy, brave and tried,
Got up in front
To bear the brunt
Of "Hobby's" mighty stride.

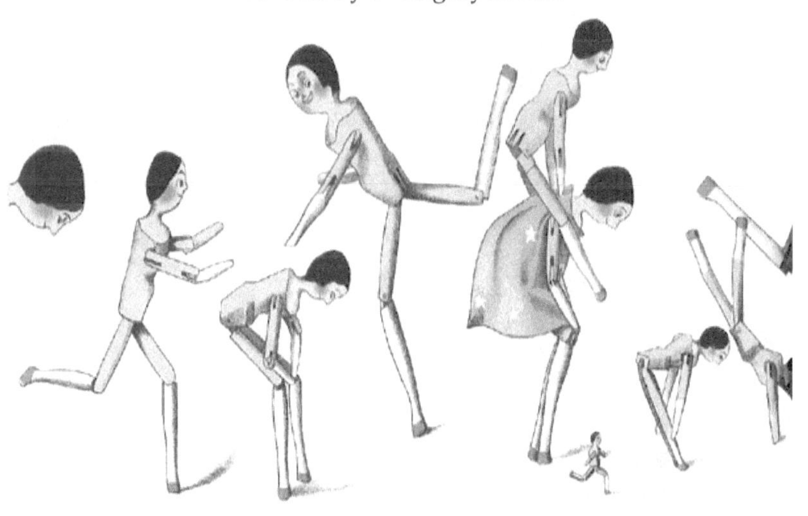

Finding a pleasant open space,
Gay Peg' unships her load;
Suggests a game
Which, it is plain,
Will soon be quite the "mode."

She tells of former Christmas nights,
When many of her kind,
At leap-frog played,
And merry made,
Fast running like the wind.

The happy moments swiftly sped
In unabated glee;
Their lungs were strong,
Their legs were long,
And supple at the knee.

But soon they hear the clock strike "two"
The hours are flying fast!
With much to do
Ere night be thro'
Its' pleasures overpast!

"Just one leap more!" cries Sarah Jane,
"This fills my wildest dream!"
E'en as she spoke,
Peg' Deutchland broke
Into a piercing scream.

Then all look round, as well they may
To see a horrid sight!
The blackest gnome
Stands there alone,
They scatter in their fright.

With kindly smile he nearer draws;
Begs them to feel no fear.
"What is your name?"
Cries Sarah Jane;
"The 'Golliwogg' my dear."

Their fears allayed--each takes an arm,
While up and down they walk;

With sidelong glance
Each tries her chance,
And charms him with "small talk".

Another wonder now attracts
The simple Sarah Jane;
Upon one knee
She drops with glee,
In case this box contain

Some pretty thing to give her joy,
Some new-discovered treat!
Old Peg', who planned
The fun in hand,
Watches with face discreet.

The lock unlatched, the lid springs up,
Knocks Sarah on her back,
With flying hair
And trying stare,
Out of the box springs "Jack".

Our naughty Peg' enjoys the scene,
Laughs long with fiendish glee;
Next takes to flight,
Gets out of sight,
Fresh tricks to plan you'll see.

Soon Sarah's heart new courage takes,
She hits upon a plan;
Makes up her mind
To run behind
And kill the staring man!

Attempts are vain, he will not die!
In terror Sarah flees;
Meets a new toy
Called "Scissors Boy",
And begs him just to please.

To help her pay bad Peggy back
For her malicious tricks;
Nor does she see
That even he
Enjoys her woeful "fix".

Peg's pious face and peaceful pose
You'd think portended fair,
When like a flash
She makes a dash,
Sends Sarah high in air!

Entangled in the "Scissors Boy",
Alas! death seems quite near;
Her trust betrayed,
This hapless maid
Sobs out her grief and fear.

'Twas Peggy's fault the whole way through;
The boy had meant no harm.
Both ran away,
Nor thought to stay
Poor Sarah's fright to calm.

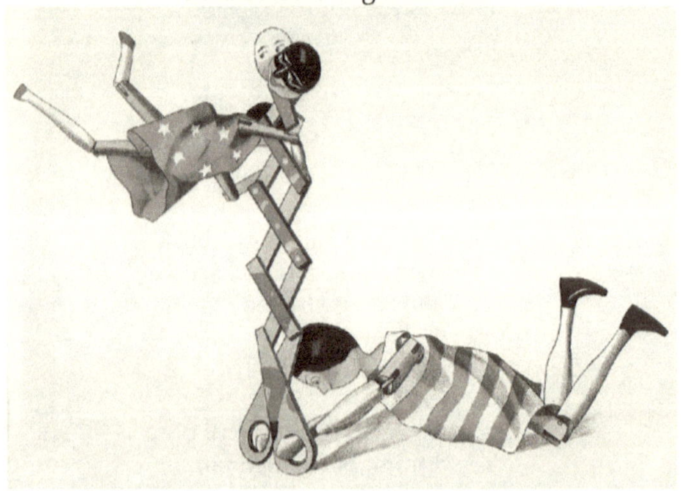

A handsome soldier passing by,
His heart quite free from guile,
With martial air
And manner rare
Soon helped the girl to smile.

He said the Ball would now begin
And begged her for a dance;
She bowed so low,
It looked as tho'
Her style had come from France.

A lively waltz the couple take,

While all admire their grace,
As round and round
Upon the ground
They spin with quickened pace.
And shameless Peg' sits on a chair
A true "flower of the wall"
While Sarah Jane,
Tis very plain,
Need never rest at all.

With graceful compliment the Clown
Bows low before the belle,

Whose modest face,
And simple grace,
In starry robe looked well.

"I know I'm but a stupid Clown,
And play a clumsy role;
Yet underneath
This painted sheath
I wear an ardent Soul."

Just then a jovial African
With large admiring eyes,
Seizes her hand
Just as the band
To give them a surprise

Strikes up the "Barn-dance"; like a flash
Both spring into their place!
Away they go
First quick, then slow,
Each movement fraught with grace.

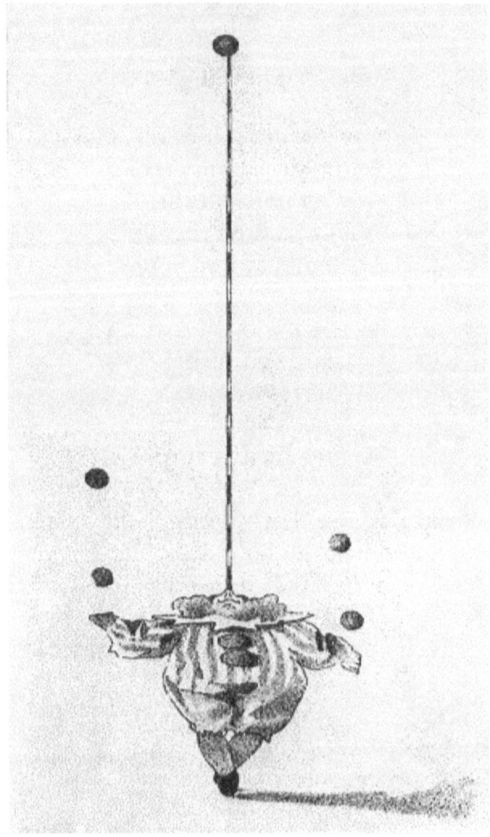

The jolly pair then pause to watch
A "Magnate" from Japan,
Who quite alone
So far from home
(Poor harmless little man)

Dances a curious Eastern dance
To many a jingling bell;
His brilliant dress,
They both confess,
Becomes him very well.

And now the Ball is at its height,
A madly whirling throng;
Each merry pair

A smile doth wear.
And Sambo sings a song.

While in their midst the artist head
Of "Golliwogg" appears,
With Peg beside,
Whose graceful stride
No criticism fears.

But even wooden limbs get tired
And want a change of play,
So "Golliwogg"
A "jolly dog"
Suggests they run away.

The big shop door is bolted fast,
But through the yard behind,
Peggy has spied
One open wide,
Which she will shortly find.

A touch--A push--and out they fly
Into the starlight night;
No one must know
The way they go
They cover up their flight.

And though their laughing faces tell

How they enjoy the fun,
No sound they make,
But quickly take
Unto their heels and run.

Nor stop until they reach a field,
And find a lovely slide;
No fear has Peg,
But Meg and Weg
Cling screaming as they glide.

The "Golliwogg" with flying hair,
Takes the first lead you see,
Nor minds at all
The "Midget" small,
Her arms outstretched in glee.

The sliders never dreamed of harm,
They sailed like ships at sea;
'Twas Meg and Weg,
Who Tripped up Peg,
And brought to grief their spree.

The wrong man often gets the blame
'Twas just so in this case,
And balls of snow
They madly throw
At "Golliwogg's" kind face.

He catches one in either eye,
And then turns tail to run;
The steady aim
Of Sarah Jane
Grows very serious fun.

He does not like the way girls act,
For five to one's not fair;
There's no escape
One hits his nape,
Another strikes his hair.

"Vengeance!" he cries, "I'll pay them out!
If girls will play with boys,
There's got be
Equality,
So here's for equipoise!"

And then some monster balls he makes,
He does not spare the snow
And as each back
Receives a whack,
Like ninepins down they go.

In life we have our "ups" and "downs",
These dolls enjoyed the same;
Though down went Weg,

Don't think, I beg,
'Twas due to Sarah Jane.

You see the sled was pretty full,
The hill was rather steep;
Weg was to steer
But in her fear
She took a backward leap.

Anon all reached the valley safe,
And skating longed to try;
The ice seemed good,
As each one stood
Upon the bank hard by.

While "Golliwogg" with cautious steps,
Toward the middle skates;
They hear a crack!
They cry, "come back
To your devoted mates!"

Too late! alas their call is vain!
He swiftly disappears!
His kind forethought
Is dearly bought,
It melts them unto tears.

But sturdy Peg is quick to act,
She gives an order clear,
"Creep on your knees,
And by degrees
We to the hole will steer."

They reach in time, Peg drags him out
With all her might and main;
Poor "Golliwogg",
A dripping log,
Must be got home again.

Behold sure signs of early dawn,
As down the field they start;
A leaden weight,
This living freight,
With faintly beating heart.

In half an hour the sun comes up,
And shows a merry face;
He winks an eye
As passing by
He sees the skating place.

And when he peeps into the shop
With jolly laughing eye,
Tho' he's not blind
He cannot find
A single toy awry!

Lector House believes that a society develops through a two-fold approach of continuous learning and adaptation, which is derived from the study of classic literary works spread across the historic timeline of literature records. Therefore, we aim at reviving, repairing and redeveloping all those inaccessible or damaged but historically as well as culturally important literature across subjects so that the future generations may have an opportunity to study and learn from past works to embark upon a journey of creating a better future.

This book is a result of an effort made by Lector House towards making a contribution to the preservation and repair of original ancient works which might hold historical significance to the approach of continuous learning across subjects.

**HAPPY READING & LEARNING!**

**LECTOR HOUSE LLP**
E-MAIL: lectorpublishing@gmail.com